Remember When

A Collection of Poems
By A Lovestruck Teen
Who Had The Courage to Dream

Sara Salam

Copyright © 2020 Sara Salam

All rights reserved. No part of this book may be used or reproduced in any manner whatsoever without written permission, except in the case of brief quotations embodied in critical articles and reviews.

ISBN: 978-1-7337263-8-2 (Paperback)
ISBN: 978-1-7337263-9-9 (eBook)

Library of Congress Control Number: 2020909853

1. Coming of Age. 2. Friendship.
3. Relationships. 4. Nature. 5. Holidays.
6. Teen—Young Adult. 7. Poetry.

Book cover design by Aspen Denita.
Author portrait by Christina Wehbe.

Printed by The Peacock Pen Press in the United States of America.

First Printing Edition 2020.

© 2020 Sara Salam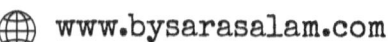

🌐 www.bysarasalam.com

📷 @bysarasalam

For those who remember when

Also by Sara Salam

My Truth Journal

Love Isn't Linear:
A Collection of Poems About Modern Love

My Newport:
A Collection of Poems About Newport Beach, CA

If Water Were Fire, A Novel

Remember When

A Collection of Poems
By A Lovestruck Teen
Who Had The Courage to Dream

Sara Salam

The Peacock Pen Press
2020

Contents

Introduction..1

Do You Realize?..3
The One..4
Our Night..5
My Miracle...6
A True Passion...7
Deepened Romance..................................8
Whenever...9
Of Fear and Trust....................................10
Our Future, Our Love, Our Belief.......11
Gone...12
Remember When......................................13
Am I?..14
A Day's Commencement.......................15
The Aid of Instinct...................................16
A Surfer's Prayer.....................................17
A Savior..18
Midnight..19
A Night Sky's Wisdom............................20
Sunset's Purpose....................................21
Life is Reborn...22
A Christmas Love....................................23
My Valentine...24
I Still Know..25
Valuables...26
I Won't Go Away......................................27
I Don't Know...28

Thank You!..31
About The Author....................................33

INTRODUCTION

I started writing poetry ...a long time ago.

I've always loved rhyme and alliteration as literary devices. I consistently find opportunities to combine words using these techniques. Appropriately, even my name is alliterative.

I also love of a good haiku.

I wrote a lot of poems my freshman and sophomore years of high school, all of which are included in this collection. At that time, I was dating a boy who shared my penchant for poetry. And so we wrote for each other and for ourselves.

The poems in this collection were all written around the turn of the millennium, between 2000 and 2004.

During this period, I became a teenager.

During this period, I was finding my voice. I built my vocabulary. I experimented with ellipses...lots of ellipses. My content focused on feeling and observation. I wrote some of my favorite poems ever during this time, like

"Gone" and this collection's title poem "Remember When."

Today, my writing still focuses on feeling and observation. It has expanded to include the complexity of how these two ideas relate to each other (and don't). In sum, introspections about the human condition.

The key difference in the process of how I create between then and now is a matter of perspective - both temporal and spatial - and hormone levels.

In my YA novel *If Water Were Fire*, which is inspired by my own high school experience, you will find a selection of these poems throughout the text - as a nod to the rawness these years of our lives are built on.

DO YOU REALIZE?

Have you ever realized
the passion I have for you?
Have you ever noticed
my eyes that somehow find you?

Have you ever seen
the smile that shines on my face?
Have you ever heard
the beats in my heart that race?

And have you ever felt
a love for someone so dear?
All you can do is pray
that they will venture near.

THE ONE

Do you see it?
I realize that now I do.
A man of a beautiful spirit
is how I'll always think of you.
Your sapphire eyes are so engaging
they melt my heart away.
and from that voice that relieves my pain
I know you're here to stay.
The smile that shines across your face
lights up my world like the blazing sun.
And from the way your hand finds mine,
I know that you're the one -
the one that gives me comfort
the one who will never go afar,
For you're the one I want to be with
to look up at the stars.

OUR NIGHT

Our night was perfect, under the stars.
Your tender eyes and bring smile healed my scars -
that represented my pain and head weakened my heart,
and through your words you whispered we would never be apart.

Your lips touched mine, in that mystical kiss,
and all that entered my mind was eternal bliss,
I know from that moment you would always be mine,
and our love could only strengthen through time.

The sunset was beautiful, just like your face;
and the walk was enchanting, in your warm embrace,
the night was one I will always remember -
one that will rest in my soul forever.

MY MIRACLE

I believe in love.
I believe in trust.

I believe in miracles...
And you are my miracle.

You are the one who lifts my spirits.
You are the one who dries my tears.
You are the one who strengthens my soul.
You are the one who dusts away from dears.

I believe in love.
I believe in trust.

I believe in miracles...
And you are my miracle.

A TRUE PASSION

The love that you give me remains shone in
    your eyes
to which all of Heaven and Earth defies.
The warmth of your embrace helps to explain
the reasons why there exists no unknown
    pain.
The smile on your face gives me the courage
    to believe
that even when there is trouble, you'll never
    leave.
The tears from my soul that have escaped my
    heart in fear
have only begun to show me when I need
    you, you will always be near.
The touch of your lips confirms our feelings of
    true passion
that with every simple kiss, our hearts have
    made a confession -
a confession that says we shall never be
    apart,
a confession that our love will always exist in
    our hearts.

DEEPENED ROMANCE

Her accent of sweetness
made him fall deeply in love.
In the depths of her heart,
she felt the same way.
Irresistible fascination
exists in each of their souls.
No words
can describe their true passion.

WHENEVER

Whenever I see you, my heart melts in anticipation.

Whenever I hug you, I feel the security you provide for my soul.

Whenever I speak to you, I hear the essence of sincerity in your soft, tender voice.

Whenever I look into your eyes, I see the spirit of the man who loves me for me.

Whenever I kiss you, I know I could never be happier.

And whenever you see me...

I hope you feel the same way.

OF FEAR AND TRUST

The love is my heart rages
like fire.
But at the same time,
it cries tears of pain.
Why is this?
A question in itself that baffles me.
Perhaps,
it comes from fear -
fear that one day
I will awake without you in my life.
or -
that someday you will find someone
better than I.
But in time,
my trust will be regained
and my forever faithful love for you
will grow stronger...
for I will love you always.

OUR FUTURE, OUR LOVE, OUR BELIEF

I can battle my weakness.
I can fight my tears.
I know I can believe in our future.
For in our future,
I see us together
never leaving each other's side.
though I fear our separation -

I believe in
Our strength,
Our courage,
And our love.

Especially our love -
for our affection is stronger
than any other aspect
of our relationship.
I love you -
that's all I need to believe.

GONE

Tears of pain stream down my face
as I think of the world I once knew.
But now
my entire universe has been altered,
because you are not in it,
You.

Your presence enriched my desire to live,
and live my life, I shall.
But now
since you have been taken away,
I will not succeed,
I will fall.

REMEMBER WHEN

Remember the day
You walked away
And left me so confused.

Remember the time
You said you were mine
And told me that I was used.

Remember the ways
You gave me praise,
And said I was yours forever.

Remember the night
When she was in sight
And when I left you forever.

AM I?

Why is it that every time I leave your embrace,
I fear pain.
It seems
I have ideas that one day
you will be gone.
Am I being unrealistic...

or do I see the inevitable future of anxiety?
Why is that every time I feel your

Lips,

I fear everlasting love.

It seems

I never want to love another, and
I risk the emotion of suffering.

Am I being selfish...
for wanting you all to myself?
I am.

A DAY'S COMMENCEMENT

As sunlight departs from our dark days of
      sorrow,
We hope it will bring back improved feelings
      tomorrow.
For the sun sets on our broken hearts and our
      shattered dreams,
This is the end of life, or so it seems.

But yet, the sun rises - and brushes away our
      tears,
For a new day is beginning without our past
      fears.
The sun's rays of light mend our soul's defeat
      and pain -
This is a new start to life, for our spirits are
      regained.

THE AID OF INSTINCT

Face eye to eye with your fears,
look at them with strength and courage.
Do not turn back.
You are too far ahead to go back now.
Your internal wisdom will guide you.
Believe in your instincts...
They will aid you through this time of challenge.
Believe in your instincts...
They will lead you to triumph and victory.

A SURFER'S PRAYER

Waves bring joy to desire
A chance to surf a set of fire.
Surfing is a dance in which the wave leads
The surfer along his dancefloor, the sea.

The sparkling, blue mass of water presents
A horizon in which hues paint dramatic
 sunsets.
The surfers look at this view as a guide
To their dreams to follow through to a
 heavenly ride.

A SAVIOR

You save peoples' lives without a question.
And watch out for those in danger.
With your instincts,
you scan the shoreline
for those in need of help.
Why do you do this?
As a favor?
As a command?
Or because it's right?
It's in your blood -
The gift of salvation.
You are a lifeguard,
You are an institution.

MIDNIGHT

It's midnight.
Stars gleam in the blanket of darkness,
surrounded by powdered clouds that reflect
the moon's shine
onto the sea that lay below.
Waves curl upon the shore as if in hiding
from the glow of the moon's presence.
Washing to and fro,
the tide climbs and falls,
weakens and strengthens.
With the moon in full,
and the star's ultra shine -
the night brightens with pride
until Dawn approaches.
Daylight comes,
and this reality
now becomes a dream.

A NIGHT SKY'S WISDOM

Flashes of light invade
the black velvet landscape
that seems to envelope the atmosphere.
Each individual speck of dust
has its own significance

and provides meaning to those who seek wisdom.
God has put these guides on this blanket of darkness
to advise the troubled

that believing in oneself is the true meaning
behind wisdom.

The night sky provides a map
for those lost
on journeys of all sorts,

that having confidence and courage
Is the concept of wisdom.

She has made these stars
to encourage those who have lost hope,
that with one simple desire and one inspiring effort,
one can accomplish a dream.

SUNSET'S PURPOSE

Blankets of light paint
a vivid portrait
of a sunset's sky,
whose soul purpose
is to create symbolical representation
of One's imagination.
The broad ranges of hues in variation
depict the originality
of each ebing's thoughts and beliefs,
as to portray the individuality
of our People.
And the clouds that evaluate
the simplicity of these visions
are the obstacles
that each person must go through
to accomplish a goal...
In the end,
this may only make the finality
more beautiful.

LIFE IS REBORN

Mist falls upon the shadows
of darkness, as if to
emphasize the sadeness present.
The clouds seem to drift
down from the Heavens
and encompass the world below.
drops of water emerge
and shower the land,
as if to rejuvenate Life,
even though it does not seem like it exists.
As the rains cease,
the Sun peers through the wall of clouds
and lights up the extinguished atmosphere
that lingered once before.
The gloom has now evaporated....

A CHRISTMAS LOVE

Mistletoe hangs, the fireplace glows -
The weather outside is bitter and cold.
But because I have you, right by my side,
I know I won't have to run and hide.

Numerous presents are visible, under the
    tree,
but all I care about is you and me.
What we share this Christmas is the only gift I
    desire,
for each time I see you my hope rises higher
    and higher.

With each Christmas wish, and each
    Christmas dream -
I know that you're the angel that as sent
    down to me.
For angels were sent from the starry heavens
    above,
And from this I know now that I am in love.

MY VALENTINE

Lips of beauty...
Warmth of fire...
Hearts of romance...
A burning desire...

A love we share so strong and bold,
Can conquer anything, and truth to told
that with such a commitment as great as ours,
It's enough to attain any limit...even something as distant as the stars.

As long days pass, and lingering nights too
I always seem to stir up a vision of you.
Your eyes so honest, and your smile so kind, I would never rather anything else take up space in my mind.

And with all of these things said and done...
I know now for certain that you are the one.

I STILL KNOW...

I still know what it feels like to be loved.
My father isn't who you think he is.
He's not some abusive dad
that when the little things disrupt his ways
He gets upset.
He's just not.
He's the kind of father that looks out for my
    well-being
and only wants the best for me.
He wants me to go to the best college in the
    world.
Sure, he may be overprotective sometimes.
But he's my father...my dad.
I still know what it feels like to be loved.
...and I only wish you could see what I see.

VALUABLES

Priceless.
Precious.
and prized.
You are all these things to me.
A privilege so generously bestowed upon me,
a wish so thankfully granted.
A dream come true for one such as little me.

Friends.
You are so valuable to me.

Emotions cannot describe
what a person you inspire me to be.

Because of you, I can be strong.
Because of you, I withhold my ambitions.

But most of all...
Because of you, I can be me.

Friends...
You build the spirit inside me.
I couldn't live without you...

You are my valuables.

I WON'T GO AWAY...

I won't go away...
...because I love you so.
I won't go away...
...because our love will only continue to grow.
I won't go away...
...because of all the trials you helped me through.
I won't go away...
...because my heart will break if I do.
I won't go away...
...because of the passion we contain.
I won't go away...
...because I know that our love will always remain.
I won't go away...
...because our hands fit together like one.
I won't go away...
...because I know that you're the one.
I won't go away...
...because our hearts are united at last.
I won't go away...
...because our love will never be a thing of the past :)

I DON'T KNOW...

I have instilled so much of my faith in you.
I don't know what to do.
All of the sudden,
This faith is gone.
I don't know what to say.
My love for you is as pure as gold.
I don't know what you see.
I thought you loved me just as true,
Please tell me baby, how can this be?
I know you need your time,
I know you need your space,
But what I don't know is...
How can I look at that gorgeous face?
...knowing it won't ever be mine?
I know I must be strong and give my heart
      time
From all of the agony and pain it does
      possess...
But either way, baby...I pray we may be
together again someday
For I LOVE YOU nonetheless.

Thank you!

I am so appreciative of you taking the time to read this collection. These poems were written during a very formative time in my life, and being able to share this period of growth and discovery with you means so much to me.

If you enjoyed Remember When, and would be willing to spare just two or three minutes...please share your review of the book on my website:

www.bysarasalam.com

Reviews help me get the book into as many hands as possible, and support my work as an author for the long-term (my dream!).

I'm grateful for your support and look forward to sharing more of my work with you!

About The Author

Sara Salam

Sara is an award-winning author and poet. Published since age 11, her writings range across fiction, nonfiction, and poetry, Sara resides in Southern California where she enjoys writing, yoga and the beach.

www.ingramcontent.com/pod-product-compliance
Lightning Source LLC
Chambersburg PA
CBHW021126080526
44587CB00010B/648